Note for Librarians: A cataloguing record for this book is available from Library and Archives Canada at www.collectionscanada.ca/amicus/index-e.html
ISBN 1-4251-0478-9

Printed in Victoria, BC, Canada. Printed on paper with minimum 30% recycled fibre. Trafford's print shop runs on "green energy" from solar, wind and other environmentally-friendly power sources.

Trafford PUBLISHING

Offices in Canada, USA, Ireland and UK

Book sales for North America and international:
Trafford Publishing, 6E–2333 Government St.,
Victoria, BC V8T 4P4 CANADA
phone 250 383 6864 (toll-free 1 888 232 4444)
fax 250 383 6804; email to orders@trafford.com
Book sales in Europe:
Trafford Publishing (UK) Limited, 9 Park End Street, 2nd Floor
Oxford, UK OX1 1HH UNITED KINGDOM
phone +44 (0)1865 722 113 (local rate 0845 230 9601)
facsimile +44 (0)1865 722 868; info.uk@trafford.com
Order online at:
trafford.com/06-2236

10 9 8 7 6 5 4 3

AMBER ROSES

AMBER ROSES

Amber roses, growing bright
in the sunshine, pure delight
so very pleasing to the eye
underneath, a crimson sky

In a garden, flowers filled
with Tulips, and some Daffodils
Marigold and Chrysanthemum
those Amber roses, out-shine each one

The roses beautiful scent, fills the air
every day, as they grow there
a more sweet smelling perfume, has'nt been invented
those Amber roses, are so scented

In the breeze, they gently sway
on a sun-filled cloudless day
all in perfect harmony
upon a hill, beneath the trees

It is there, I like to spend an hour
just relaxing, among the flowers
pretty sights and pretty smells
in that garden, I often dwell

When I want to ease my mind
in the sunny summer time
it is to that place, that I do go
where, those Amber roses grow.

THE MEMORIES OF A DYING SOLDIER

As l lie here today, upon this cold cold clay
while a battle rages, all around
any time, from now on, l know they'll come along
to take me to be buried in the ground

There's a burning in my heart, and it's true that l must part
from this world, so very soon
but before l die, I'd like to say goodbye
to all my comrades, in my shattered, platoon

lt does'nt seem so long ago, since l wanted to be a hero
back, when l was a lad at school
l always fancied the army life, some how, it just seemed right
though my friends told, me, I'm a fool

Still, l was recruited one day, and l trained right away
though sometimes, l found the going, so tough
but the boss man said, get tough, or you are dead
cause a battle field, can be bloody, and rough

Shortly after, we got the call, our platoon one and all
were to be sent, to this war torn land

though somewhat apprehensive, at the start
but with hand on heart
l was willing, to take a stand

We were thrown in, at the deep end

and l lost many friends
much, to numerous to tell
as we continue to fight, l have seen some horrible sights
in this place,which is just a living hell

l was caught up, in a blast
now my time on earth, will soon have past
and l'll be returning home, one of these days
they'll play the Last Post,at my grave
and say l was so brave
as they bury,me beneath the cold cold clay.

A FOOLISH MAN

I sold my tv to buy a car
but l did'nt get very far
so l sold my funiture, tables and chairs
still l did'nt get any where

Then l sold my cutlery, cups and plates
to sell them, l did not hesitate
l sold the pictures from off the walls
l just went, and sold them all

Next, l even sold my very bed
l had nowhere to lay my head
in the end, l sold the kitchen sink
and then l stopped and had a drink

l drank and drank and drank some more
cause l had lots of money, galore
but l drank all my money away
and so at home, l had to stay

Cause l still, did'nt have a car outside my door
l did'nt have a chair, l had to sit on the floor
no table, upon which to dine
l had wasted my money on whiskey and wine

l did'nt have any cutlery,cups or plates
to get them back, it was much too late
no bed, upon which to sleep
l had to lie in the corner, like a tired old sheep
Gone, were my pictures and tv
l had nothing to look, at, nothing to see
without the sink, my kitchen looked bare

there was nothing left, any where

Still, I wanted to buy a car
cause without, one I could'nt go far
I sold the books from off the self
that was'nt enough, so I had to sell myself

Put a notice in the paper,For sale,Man
who is quite willing to lend a helping hand
he'll wash the dishes, and wash your teeth
keep your house,so nice and neat

He'll cut the grass, and cut your hair
clean the pictures, and clean the air
walk the child and walk the dog
cut the turf, down in the bog

He'll scrub the floor, and scrub the sink
but don't ever, offer him a drink
cause he'd drink and drink all night and day
and he'd drink all his money away

But he's quite willing to do any thing,
I sat and waited, for my phone to ring
I waited and waited, for weeks on end
after that, I waited again

Still, I waited for someone to call
but no one bothered, to phone at all
and so, today here I am
a lonely empty, foolish man.

A SELF-EXPLANATORY DAY

It was a self-explanatory kind of day
as it did'nt need any explaining
rain was falling from the sky
therefore it was raining
a cold north wind did blow
so the wind was blowing
and later on snow fell to the ground
therefore it started snowing

l arose in the morn of that day
so l arose in the morning
then l started to yawn
therefore l took to yawning
l got something to eat
so l did some eating
there was some one l wanted to meet
therefore l hoped to have a meeting

When l went out onto the street, the wind did freeze
so the wind was freezing
then l started to sneeze
therefore l took to sneezing
l met a postman delivering letters
those letters he was delivering
l felt so cold, l did shiver
so l was shivering

In the distance l heard a church bell ring
so the bell was ringing
and l listened to a robin sing
so the bird was singing
l walked further on down the street

so l kept on walking
two men at the corner stood and talked
therefore those men were talking

Women bought some items in a shop
so they were shopping
but l did'nt have time to stop
so l had'nt time for stopping
l passed a railway station, just as a train did leave
so the train was leaving
and a lover, for her departing boyfriend did greive
therefore she was greiving

When at last, l got to, where my friend, l was to meet
so the place, where l was to have my meeting
l sat down on a park seat
therefore l sat on the seating
my friend and l did converse
so we had a conversation
and that is how l was situated
therefore that was my situation

As l was returning home
so as l was homeward bound
snow started to fall
snowflakes fell to the ground.

AFTER DARK

After dark, when the sun goes down
after work, we can hit the town
have a drink, and just relax
.life is short, you've got to live it to the max

We could go up, to the Country Inn
and sip a beer, or maybe a gin
tell a joke, and sing a song
meet our friends, and they can sing along

If we are feeling hungry, before going to the pub
we could call at the Village Diner, and buy some grub
eat a meal, and tip the waiter
then when we are full, have a drink later

There's a jukebox in the corner, and it never stops
it plays all kinds of music, from country to pop
a little jazz, and some soul
but best of all, it plays Rock and Roll

My feet are really tapping,when listening to Chuck Berry
that Rock and Roll sound, has me feeling merry
and I'm always good and jolly
when hearing Elvis, or Buddy Holly

We could sit a while, and have a chat
draw funny faces, on the table mats
and later on, when Time, is called
we will go back home, after all.

ANOTHER MAN

She has got, another man
that, was'nt in my plans
but l saw her hold his hand
in town, last night
there was a smile upon her face
he had his arm around her waist
and l think it's a disgrace
it just is'nt, right

Call me a sentimental fool
but she has broken all the rules
today l saw them walking along the Strule
down by the river
he even gave her a kiss
and though she will be missed
the situation is this
l just can't forgive her

Now she is by his side
to stay with him, she has decided to decide
I'm, like a wrecked ship, floating on the tide
cause l have gone to pieces
she has cast my love away
now that with him, she is going to stay
this lonliness I'm feeling every day
like the wind, increases

But there is nothing l can do
like the sky, l am so blue
cause her and l are through
l understand
they say that love is blind

and I cannot see, why she left me behind
in order just to find
another man.

AS I RECALL

As l recall, we were quiet small
whenever first we met
and though it's true, over the years we grew
we're not gaints yet
but even so, our love did grow
just like the garden flowers
and all along, it has stayed strong
there's no love as strong as ours

As l recall, you played football
with the boys at school
and you knew, it was'nt a girls thing to do
but you liked, to break the rules
you played hard, in the school yard
though you were always fair
and it was one day, when l watched you play
that l first saw you there

As l recall, behind the school wall
is where,we first kissed
you looked your best, in your bright red dress
and a bracelet on your wrist
we were all alone, then l walked you home
and you held my hand
l felt so good, cause l knew l would
always be your man

As l recall, the old dance hall
years later, l would frequent
and it's true, it was with you
that l always went
we'd dance along, to every song

all around the floor
then at the end of the night, in the bright moon light
I'd leave you to your door

As I recall, it was Father Mc Fall
who married, us on our wedding day
and it's true, the words I do
to you, I did say
but I know, that was long ago
how the time does fly
after all we've been through, me and you
will never, say goodbye.

AS

As far as the eye can see
as far as the ear can hear
as far as away as the mountains
as far away as next year
as deep as the deepest ocean
as deep as the raging sea
as long as the world keeps turning
can man really be free?

As high as the sky above
as high as a bird in flight
as high as someone on drugs
as high as a golden kite
as wise as the wise old owl
as wise as the wisest king
as sure as death itself
there will always be suffering

As black as the blackest night
as black as the black hole
as black as the lonely blackbird
as black as a piece of coal
as clear as spring water
as clear as a summers day
it is clearly plain to see
that life, in this world, is just a short stay.

BESIDE

Beside a church, beside a shop
beside a train, which does'nt stop
beside a river,that rapidly flows
and gazing at an amazing rainbow

Beside water, as it cascades down a fall
on crashing to the bottom, making a thunderous call
beside a city center fountain
or a snow capped mountain

Beside a forest full of trees
or a colony of bees
beside a castle built on high
it's towers reaching for the sky

Beside a herd of running deer
they look so elegant
or a beautiful swan,
it's neck, long, and bent

Beside a mightly elephant
or busy little ants
beside a dog that always barks
even a great white shark

Beside a garden full of flowers
in the sunshine showers
beside a gaint oak tree
beside you, beside me.

BUTTERFLY

Butterfly, fly away, bring me back a tune
let it be a sweet melody,
that I can sing beneath the shinning moon
shinning moon, so bright, with your soft moonbeams
shine upon my bed, and brighten up my dreams

Sweet dreams, come to me, so I'll wake up with a smile
then I will be happy, I'll walk a country mile
country mile, though long you are, take me to a field
where flowers grow, and rivers flow, and a fiddler plays a reel

Fiddler, play a happy song, so I'll be feeling merry
I'll close my eyes, and find myself, dancing with the faries
little faries, bring me luck, beside a fairy tree
take me to the rainbows end, and a pot of gold, I'll see

Pot of gold, all aglow, you will bring me pleasure
and every where I go, I'll have lots of treasure
treasure trail, lead me to where, peaceful waters flow
where people live in harmony, and seeds of love they sow

Seeds, produce a tender crop
like angels in the sky
good things to see, like honey bees
and little butterflies.

CARRYING WATER IN A COLANDER

Asking a drunkard, a sensible question
and expecting a sensible reply
is like carrying water in a colander
hoping to stay dry

Holding a very hungry baby
and telling it not to cry
is like carrying water in a colander
hoping to stay dry

Trusting a hibitual lier
to tell the truth, and not to lie
is like carrying water in a colander
hoping to stay dry

Walking unprotected, through a desert storm
thinking sand, won't get in your eyes
is like carrying water in a colander
hoping to stay dry

Jumping off the edge of a cliff
in order to unaided, fly
is like carrying water in a colander
hoping to stay dry

Taking the battery out of a battery clock
so that time, won't pass by
is like carrying water in a colander
hoping to stay dry

On a dark and cloudy day
looking up, to see a clear blue sky

is like carrying water in a colander
hoping to stay dry

Telling pigs,to be clean and tidy
in a dirty pig sty
is like carrying water in a colander
hoping to stay dry

Expecting to live forever
and never ever die
is like carrying water in a colander
hoping to stay dry

CHANGE THAT RECORD MAGGIE

Change that record, Maggie
I've heard that one before
I'm getting tired of listening to it
do'nt want to hear it anymore
it's making my head spin
as it spins around
so change that record, Maggie
cause it's bringing me down

Put on some decent music
play another song
and as we sit by the fire
I just might sing along
I have travelled far to get here
journeyed manys a mile
my visit will be short
as I can only stay a while

On my way here, the night was dark and lonely
as lonely as could be
a ghostly kind of wind
was whispering in the trees
the moon did'nt show it's face
all the stars must have ran out of gas
the road was long and winding
and I tried to get here fast

Many summers have passed by
since last we met
I've been to distant lands
but I've got no regrets
I crossed so many oceans

wide and deep and blue
still no matter where I roamed
I remembered you

Been to so many places
seen so many sights
met so many people
both black and white
but no matter where I went
no matter where I roamed
I still longed for the day
when I'd be going home

So I have come here to see you
now that I have returned
I'm sitting by your fire
as it brightly burns
you have welcomed me back
from across the sea
with some music playing
and some cake and tea

But I wish you'd change that record
you've been playing it all night long
put on something different
play another song
I know all the words by now
from front to back
so change the record Maggie
or I'll be making tracks.

CHILLY IN CHILE

It's chilly in Chile, and sunny in Spain
there's rain in Romania, l won't go back there, again
l ran in lran, and bought a rack in lraq
then bought china in China, it is white and black

I climbed a pole in Poland
and got grease in Greece
l saw turkeys in Turkey, but did'nt see, any geese
l was hungry in Hungry, and in Bulgaria, saw a bull
then rang a bell in Belguim, it had a rope to pull

l was rushing, in Russia
and in the Czech Republic, wrote a cheque
l slipped on ice, in Iceland, and hurt my neck
l bought sweets in Sweden
then in Scotland, drank a Scotch
the wind was howling in Holland
in Switzerland, l purchased a Swiss watch

l phoned Libby, in Libya
and ate Brazil nuts,in Brazil
l watched Columbo,in Columbia
then took a stand, in Afghanistan, and l'm standing, still
l met Jordan, in Jordan, and Sue, in the Sudan
l had a new feeling, in New Zealand
then went back home to Iris, in the Irish land.

DO'NT

Do'nt smoke in bed, or you could wake up dead
when you are drinking, do'nt get drunk
do'nt worry too much, about such and such
there's no need to live like a monk

Do'nt walk on walls, off, which you might fall
or drive over the edge of a cliff
do'nt spend your time, on railway lines
cause when a train comes, you'll have to shift

Do'nt hang around with fools, who break the rules
it's better to keep on the right side of the law
and when you cut wood, you really should
try to use a saw

Do'nt stand in the rain, cause you'll be having pains
whenever you catch the cold
do'nt lie too long in the sun, or your skin will burn
and wrinkle, and you'll look so old

Do'nt idolize orthers, cause they won't bother
to idolize you
do'nt have any heros, or you'll feel you're a zero
and then you'll be feeling blue

Do'nt get too down hearted, if your day has'nt started
the way you hoped, that it would
do'nt be pessimistic, but be optimistic
and everything will turn out good.

EATING MY WORDS

I'm eating my words cause I'm hungry
said things I should'nt have said
still, the words all taste fine
as they are all mine
each of them came out of my head

I've bitten some humble pie
and not just a slice or two
but at least I admit it
that I have bit it
and even admit it to you

I've had to swallow my pride
and pride goes before a fall
I have fallen down
want to be swallowed up by the ground
now. for once and for all

I 'm walking the road to nowhere
and nowhere is where I am bound
I'm getting there fast,
like I've done in the past
there's plenty of nowhere around

I'm sleeping on a bed of nothing
and nothing. is what I have got
I've got no bedclothes
from my head to my toes
I'm as naked as the sun, when it's hot

I'm seeking a little forgiveness
though where to find,it I just don't know

forgive and forget,
but some forget to forgive
I'm still looking, high and low

I'm drowning in an empty ocean
but nobody, can hear my pleas
I'm quickly going under
and being to wonder
why no one, is rescuing me

I'm floating on a cloud in the sky
sailing towards the moon
I can touch all the stars
but the moon still looks far
I'm longing to get there soon

I'm climbing a mountain of hope
and hoping not to fall
I need a good grip,
so, not to slip
as this mountain I'm climbing is tall

I'm playing my tune in the wind
but the wind is carrying my tune away
perhaps I'll get it back again
whenever there is rain
without my tune,I can't play

I'm banging my head against a brick wall
which is making my head feel sore
but I'm not getting through
no matter what I do
I just find an open door

I'm here in the middle of a dream
dreaming of rainbows so bright
while sharing my dream with you
there is just one more thing to do
and that, is to say goodnight.

FISHERMAN ON A BIKE

Fisherman on a bike
are you going to catch some pike
on your bike, with your fishing rod
perhaps you are going to catch some cod

Fisherman on a bike
what kind of fish do you like?
if your favourite is sardines
you won't get any in a stream

Fisherman on a bike
be your name, Jim or Mike
or do they call you Fisherman Joe?
as on your bike, to the river you go

Fisherman on two wheels
maybe you are going to catch some eels
don't forget, you'll need some bait
to catch fish, for your dinner plate

Fisherman on two wheels
do you cross many feilds
on your way to the river
hoping your fishing rod will deliver

Fisherman on two wheels
I wonder just how do you feel
as you cycle on your own
the fish you catch, how do you take them home?

Fisherman on two wheels
do you cook your own meals

when you return home on your bike
or could there be, a fishermans wife?

GETTING ON A BIT

He is getting on, a bit
his hair, is growing thin
there is less hair upon his head
and more upon his chin
below his hairline,
wrinkles cover his brow
cause he is getting on a bit now

He has really slowed down
as he walks, at a snails pace
these days he has bother
bending down to tie each shoe lace
when he was young
he used to be so fit
but now those days are gone
and he is getting on a bit

His teeth have fallen out
and his face has fallen in
there is now an empty gap
between his nose and chin
his face resembles a damaged car
which has been badly hit
his appearance has changed
since he's been getting on a bit

His bones make a creaking sound
like a creaking old chair
they go snap crackle and pop
just about every where
his memory has gone
whatever became of it

things start to go
when you are getting on a bit

His eyesight is deteriorting
he is going for another eye test
you could safely say
his eyesight is not the best
upon the opticians chair
he will be glad to sit
to rest his weary bones
cause he is getting on a bit

He is like a tired old workhorse
which has been put out to graze
like a well worn shirt
which has seen better days
like a burnt-out candle
which can no longer be lit
and so to sum him up
he is getting on a bit.

GOOSEBERRY JAM

Gooseberry jam, eggs and ham
and a slice or two of bacon
beans on toast, a Sunday roast
are'nt things to be forsaken
winding country roads, croaking toads
add a touch of spring
Dandelion wine, songs that rythme
make the heart want to sing

A rainbow in the sky,kites on high
above the evergreens
children at play, on a summers day
beside a sleeply little stream
Goldfish in a bowl, stories told
about pirates on the seas
sitting in the evening sun, with a coconut bun
and a cup of freshly made tea

Windmills which turn, milk in a churn
brightly coloured paper planes
thorns and brambles, a quiet little ramble
up a roaming, hilltop lane
a galaxy of stars, trains going far
along a lonesome track
birds on the wing, as Nightingales sing
sunshine on your back

Dreams comming true, meeting friends you knew
and some you still know
bowing out in style, with a happy smile
what a way to go.

HOME TO STAY

Home to stay,l've been away too long
l went from right to wrong
sung a worried song
don't know how l carried on
but now l'm home to stay

Home to stay, l did what l have done
been held-up at the point of a gun
l watched the setting sun
now all my wars have been won
so now l'm home to stay

Home to stay, l've had so many fears
shed a thousand tears
had some lonely years
but now the way is clear
and l am home to stay

Home to stay, l've walked a hundred roads
had no home abode
carried a weary load
l've seen more than l've showed
but now l'm home to stay

Home to stay, l have crossed feilds of green
and quiet country streams
but no matter where l've been
l have always dreamed
of being home to stay

Home to stay, l've seen so many sights
fought some bitter fights

lived through the darkest nights
so now it's only right
that I am home to stay.

I'II SEE YOU WHEN I SEE YOU

I'II see, you when l see, you
said the fisherman to the fish,
and the next time l see, you
you'll be sitting on my dish
he almost caught, it on that warm summers day
but it was the old familar story
of the one that got away

l'll see, you when l see,you
said the beggerman to the theif
as they parted company
on a cold and wind-swept street
the theif just motioned with his hand
cause he had'nt much to say
the beggerman did'nt know that the theif had stolen his money
before, he walked away

l'll see, you when l see, you
said the jockey to the horse
it was the jockey's first race
and he was glad, that he completed the course
he was surprised, that on the horses back, he managed to stay
and he felt a sense of satisfaction
as he walked away

l'll see, you when l see, you
said the wife to her man
he was off to fight in battle
in some distant land
he promised, he would return, victorious, some day

then she waved to him from the harbour
as his boat sailed away

I'll see, you when I see, you
said the son to his departed mother
there were tears in his eyes
cause he loved her like no orther
he stood by her grave
as she was buried beneath the clay
then he said a prayer in silence
when the mourners had gone away.

NOT FINISHED YET

Life, for me has been cruel
it has dealt me many blows
there have been lots of times
when l have felt so low
life has knocked me down
but up, l always get
cause like a battered boxer
l'm not finished yet

Even in those times
when life had me on the ropes
l did'nt throw in the towel
l never gave up hope
at times, l have been sore and tired
and ultimately, upset
but no matter what life throws at me
l'm not finished yet

l have been down and out
at my wits end
and in times of trouble
l could not find a friend
the odds have been stacked against me
l could'nt win a bet
they say that l'm a loser
but l'm not finished yet

l'm nothing, if not a fighter
l never do give up
and l have drunk the poison
out of life's bitter cup
and even though l'm bruised

what life has taught, me l won't forget
l might be worn and weary
but l'm not finished yet

So if, you come my way
just take, me as l am
l'm my own person
l am, my own man
and now you know the truth
what you see, is what you get
l am a true survivor
cause l'm not finished yet.

IF I HAD A MILLION

If l had a million, l would be a millionair
if l had a billion, l would'nt have a care
lf l had a fortune, l would be fortunate
but, as it is, l'm at povertys gate

I dream of being rich, but dreaming is all l do
l'm like a single lonesome cloud
on an endless sky of blue
slowly drifting by, a lost and lonely soul
but if, l had a million, l'd have friends untold

Like a fish out of water, l feel l don't belong
like a down and out singer, who has ran out of songs
l'm doing my best, to keep the wolves from my door
but if l had a million, l would have money galore

There's a raindrop on my window, and a teardrop in my eye
there's an aching in my heart, but l do'nt know why
the reason could be, due to my lack of money
but if l had a million, all my days would be sunny

lf l had a fortune, l would'nt seek any fame
all l really want, is not to want again
l would be so happy, just to have everything l need
but if l had a million, l could join the elite.

IF MIRRORS HAD'NT OF BEEN INVENTED

If mirrors had'nt of been invented
how could people tell
whether or not, they are looking well?
they'd never see their face
just like a bird in the sky
and the lack of mirrors
would be the reason why

If mirrors had'nt of been invented
what would women do
when putting on eye shadow, be it black or blue?
and how would they apply lipstick,pink or red?
without mirrors, they'd have to guess, instead

If mirrors had'nt of been invented
how would men begin
to shave the hairs, from off their cheeks and chin
without a mirror, at which to stand and stare
how would men know
whether or not, they left any hairs?

If mirrors had'nt of been invented
driving, would be hell
without rear view mirrors, and door mirrors as well
there would be more accidents, and more deaths too
if mirrors, had'nt of been invented
what would we do

But we take them all for granted
of that, there is no doubt
though how would we manage

if there were none about?
they would be badly missed, by women, and men too
if mirrors had'nt of been invented
just what, would we do?

IF THE WEATHER HOLDS

If the weather holds
and rain does'nt fall
and strong winds do'nt up-root
trees which are tall
and the earth does'nt shake
like a leaf on a tree
and ships are'nt wrecked
on stormy seas

And lightening does'nt strike
and thunder does'nt roar
and the sky does'nt grow dark
like never before
and animals don't run for shelter
though they cannot be saved
and headstones don't fall
upon every grave

And the moon does'nt dance
like it's on fire
and the sound of the wind
does'nt grow higher and higher
and large black clouds
across, the tortured sky, don,t race
and rooves of houses
do'nt go flying all over the place

And birds in the air
are'nt blowen about, like paper planes
and the earth is'nt drowned
under a deluge of rain
and bridges don't collapse

into rivers so high
and even laughing Hyenas
don't begin to cry
and cities are'nt in darkness
cause the power has failed
and prisoners do'nt escape
from unguarded jails

And mountains don't tumble
like houses built with playing cards
and workmans huts
aren't tossed about like tin cans, in council yards
and volcanos don't erupt
and the earth does'nt melt
and the full force of nature
does'nt really be felt
and forests everywhere
don't go on fire
untill the glowing flames
can't reach any higher

And crops in the fields
are'nt all washed away
like grains of sand
all along the bay
till singers can't sing
and thinkers can't think
and the whole world around us
just appears to shrink
and scientists run out of answers
and husbands run out of wives
and something strange
is'nt running our lives

And mankind is'nt gripped
by anxiety and fear
when all the lights have gone out
so nothing is clear
till everything is wrong
therefore nothing is right
and death comes a calling
like a thief in then night
so, if the weather holds
let's go for a walk, tomorrow.

JOHNNY PICK YOUR NOSE

They called him, Johnny Pick Your Nose
cause that is what he did
he used to pick his nose
sometimes they'd call him,Snotty Sid
he had a bad habit, of picking his nose
and he did'nt have a hanky
so he would use his clothes

He came from a rough part of town
his family were quite poor
just how many brothers and sisters he had
nobody was too sure

He was the butt of many jokes, in the school yard
and he just could'nt ignore, them
though he tried so hard
they say he was'nt smart
he was considered thick
orther boys would draw two noses
and ask, him which, one he wanted to pick

He ran away from home
when he was just fourteen years old
and went looking for a job
in the rain and cold
he got a job as a newspaper boy
delivering papers on a bike
the money was'nt great
but it was a job he liked

The newspaper firm later gave him an office job
when he became eighteen

because of him being a good worker
and, he was so keen
he worked his way to the top
and now he wears the finest clothes
but yet he still remembers the time
when he was called, Johnny Pick Your Nose.

LET'S DO A RUNNER

Let's do a runnner, and get away
to where we go, is where we'll stay
we'll tell nobody that we are going
so they will have, no way of knowing

Let's do a runner in the night
and we'll be gone. by morning light
we'll slip away, as time slips by
and disappear, just you and l

With nothing to lose and much to gain
we'll see the sun, forget the rain
and we can roam so wild and free
nobody else, just you and me

Cause there's a world to explore
and it's right there, outside the door
once we are gone, we won't slow down
when we hit the road,and get out of town

With no ties to hold us back
just like a train upon a track
we'll be rolling along,on down the line
alone together, feeling fine

Though our pockets are full of empty, devoid of any doe
we'll manage somehow, that much l do know
with our minds empty of fear, and our hearts full of hope
where there's a will, there's a way and l know we can cope

Maybe we'll hitch a ride on a passing truck
and tell the driver, we are down on our luck
or on the run from some crazy cop
tell him to keep going, not to stop

We'll be as free as the wind, with the wind in our hair
where the road takes us,we'll be going there
just following our nose no maps or plans
like a bird in the sky, looking down on the land

Nobody knows, what lies ahead
so let's live a life,before we're dead
get a piece of the action, while we're still able
breaking free, like a horse, bolting out of the stable

Let's take whatever is going, while the going is good
I truly think, we really should
the world is our oyster,let's get a taste
and time is something, not to waste

Life is an adventure, to be lived to the full
but if we are not adventurous, life will be dull
so let's do a runner, and break free
nobody else, just you and me.

LIFE IN THE OLD DOG YET

Crowds gathered along the race track
and the scene was set
all eyes focused on Slimline Joe
cause there's life in the old dog yet

Countless money exchanged hands
as punters placed their bets
Slimline Joe was the hot favourite
cause there's life in the old dog yet

Many years of running are behind him
many cups, in his throphy cabinet, have been set
he is a true champion
and there's life in the old dog yet

He was by far the oldest greyhound there that night
but still, his owner did'nt fret
Ambrose Martin was confident, that Slimline Joe would win
cause there's life in the old dog yet

At last, the race started
and that hare, the dogs tried to get
Slimline Joe set off at a lighting pace
for there's life in the old dog yet

Already, punters who backed orther, dogs
were starting to have regrets
as Slimline Joe, showed them the way
cause there's life in the old dog yet

He ran round the track, at breakneck speed

the night, was cool and wet
a number one, was on his back
and there's life in the old yet

When Slimline Joe won by a mile
Ambrose Martin, was so proud of his pet
another race, another cup
cause there's life in the old dog yet.

MAY AS WELL

You may, as well come on over
you may as well stay awhile
and we will be so happy, we may, as well smile
we may, as well have a party
and all our friends, we can tell
so if, they want to come along
then they may as well

We may, as well play some music
we may as well sing a song
and if, our friends care, to
they may as well sing along
and when our party is going good
when, we are feeling swell
we will drink a toast, to all our friends
because we may as well

We may, as well have some fun
we may as well, play some games
and if, the games are going fine
we may as well play again
we could have a go at a game
where we can buy and sell
and if, you think you can win
then, you may as well

Our party could last for hours
and time, will slip away
you may as well stay for as long as you like
for as long as you want to stay
but when it is time for the orthers, to go
l, will ring my bell

and if we want to do it all again at a later date
then, we may as well.

MINI HANS MAKES LIGHTS THAT WORK

Mini Hans makes lights that work
at his factory in Berlin
lights green and red, I've heard it said
nobody makes lights as goòd as him

He works away, each and every day
morning, noon and night
such a dedicated worker
making all those wonderful lights

Car lights, traffic lights
lights for Christmas trees
bright lights, white lights
are all made by he

Mini Hans can make lights
for almost any occasion
even lights for birthday cakes
and wedding invitations

Big, lights small, lights
lights, both round and square
at his factory in Berlin
Mini makes them there

And his lights, light up the world
from Munich, to Montreal
anywhere, in any street
Mini, made them all

Everywhere around the globe

his lights have been sighted
that's because, each and every customer, of his
is absolutely, delighted.

MORE OR LESS

A roomless house,a homeless door
a single pebble on a distant shore
a faceless picture hanging on an open wall
a lonesome star, waiting to fall

A motherless child, on an endless street
in a wayward town, with nobody to meet
a mindless mind,with thoughts for no one
an early bird in the morning sun

A careless driver , who just does'nt care
on a hedgeless road, going nowhere
a pointless sign, which never helps
a speechless pup, unable to yelp

A charmless charm, just dangling down
an expressionless face, which neither smiles nor frowns
a characterless character, showing no emotion
a bottomless well, as deep as the ocean

A pennyless man, without any money
a jokeless comedian, trying to be funny
a songless singer, who has ran out of tunes
a hungry fox howling at the moon

A moonless night, as black as coal
an ageless person, neither young nor old
a colourless liquid, as clear as could be
on a winters day, a leafless tree

A hopeless case, devoid of any hope

a helpless mother, unable to cope
a legless chair, a wheeless car
which goes no where, near or far

A priceless gift, which money can't buy
a flightless bird, unable to fly
a toeless sock,or a heeless shoe
fingerless gloves, with fingers sticking through

A sleepless night, which never ends
a stampless letter, which no one sends
an inkless pen, that has just ran dry
a perfect time, to say goodbye.

MY AMBITION IN LIFE

My ambition in life, is to get me a wife
who will cook and sew
and every day, she would say, how much she loves me
so
we would never argue, and definitely, not fight
for to me, that would be
my ambition in life

My ambition in life, is to have lots of money
always have plenty of doe
so l would have money to spend
every where l'd go
then l could buy some pretty things
for, my lovely wife
and to me, that would be
my ambition in life

My ambition in life, is to go, on a great world cruise
if l had lots of money, that's what l would do
happy would l be,sailing on the sea
along, with my wonderful wife
for to me, that would be, my ambition in life

My ambition in life, is to write a book
which would go to the top
and low and behold, it would be sold
in every book shop
then everyone would know, me
and they'd know my wife
for to me, that would be
my ambition in life

My ambition in life, is to retire to the country
when my working days, are at an end
and though it would be peaceful and quiet, there
I would still, have many friends
and when my days are numbered
on my headstone, they would write,
Here Lies A Most Contented, Man
He Achieved All, His Ambitions In Life.

MY FAVOURITE CHAIR

I'm taking my time, cause l'm going no where
and l'm in no hurry to get there
how long it takes, l do'nt really care
cause l'm sitting relaxing, on my favourite chair

l'm scratching my head,and thinking things through
for there is'nt much else to do
if there is, l am not aware
so l'm sitting relaxing, on my favourite chair

There's a cat on my window sill, it is looking in
it is walking back and forth, making such a din
black and white, are the colours of it's hair
still l'm relaxing, on my favourite chair

Got my feet by the fire, and my shoes by the door
and l want to stay here forever more
the sound of Sinatra, fills the air
as l'm sitting relaxing, on my favourite chair

On my mantlepiece,stands a picture of a girl l once knew
but then she told, me that we were through
in life, nothing is fair
so l'm sitting relaxing, on my favourite chair

Now l'm free and single, my time is my own
and listening to Sinatra, l do'nt feel alone
l'm enjoying, myself really, l swear
sitting relaxing on my favourite chair

The sun has gone down, the moon has arose

outside my window, the cold wind blows
autumn leaves are falling, they are everywhere
as I'm sitting relaxing, on my favourute chair

But here inside, I'm as snug as a bug
and having a sip, out of my whiskey jug
since I'm on my own, I do'nt need to share
sitting relaxing, on my favourite chair

The night has arrived,another day has gone by
I'm thinking to myself how time does fly
for whatever tomorrow throws, at me, I am prepared
in the meantime, I'm relaxing on my favourite chair.

NEVER BEEN DRUNK IN MY LIFE

I have never beeen drunk in my life
you can ask my mother or wife
l intend to stay sober till my life is over
some tell me that is'nt right

But l do like to smoke
though it makes me splutter and choke
it is bad, l know that's true
but what else can l do?
this coughing, sure is'nt a joke

l really eat a lot of food
my appetite, sure is good
it's like feeding buns to a bear
but l don;t really care
l'd eat the bear too, if only l could

Sometimes l rift and l fart
but l've been like that from the start
they say. that l'm impolite
but l don't give a slight
it just means l have got a good heart

When l'm angry, l've been known to curse
but there are things much worse
l'd swear blind, like a donkeys behind
l was five, when l started it first

l often get into a fight
on a Saturday night
my fists do go flying
and leave some poor devil crying

some say, what l do is not right

l have even dabbled in cocaine
it had a funny effect on my brain
l felt strange in the head
l thought l was dead
so l won't be doing that again

But l have never been drunk in my life
you can ask my mother or ex- wife
she left me one day
saying she could'nt stay
because of my, smoking,farting, heavy eating
rifting cursing drug taking, ect,
so she left, after we had a fight.

NOREEN

Her face was fresh and freckled
like a butterfly, speckled
l really only knew her for a while
she was always full of fun
as bright as the morning sun
and she had a Mona Lisa, kind of smile

She was as cheerful as a cherry
even in February
that was the month, in which we met
it was on Valentines, she really looked so fine
and l can still picture, her yet

She had a dainty little nose
and she used to paint her toes
sometimes she'd paint her finger nails to match
she wore a bracelet on her arm
and she kept a lucky charm
but for some reason, she never wore a watch

She asked me for the time
in a pub, on Valentines
l told her it was time, for me to go
though l never saw her before
when l walked out the door
she was standing, there in the winter snow

So l left her home
as she was all alone
plus, she was as frozen as a bag of Birds Eye peas
when she invited me in
she offered me gin

but I told, her I'd rather have a cup of tea

I next met her again
in the summer rain
she said to me, I've seen your face somewhere before
she had a bright umbrella
and another fella and I never saw her after that, anymore.

OLD BOOTS

Old boots, old leather
they have seen, all kinds of weather
sun, rain, hail and snow
but now they don't have anywhere to go

Old boots, with missing boot laces
they've been to so many places
pounding the roads for so long
now they are lying, there looking forlorn

Old boots,discarded
it's been a while, since their first journey started
then, they were shiny and new
but now, they have nothing to do

Old boots, lying about
they have seen better days, no doubt
the uppers are parting from the soles
which in turn,are peppered with holes

Old boots,about which nobody cares
like a worn- out tyre, threadbare
their days are numbered, unlike the miles they've done
and now, not of use to any one

Old boots, now they are not so tough
like a beaten-up boxer, feeling rough
every dog has it's day
every boot,gets thrown away.

ONE MAN AND HIS DOG

One man and his dog, on a country road side
thumbing a lift, trying to hitch a ride
hoping someone will stop, but the cars all go by
still, one man and his dog, determinedly try

One man and his dog, standing in the rain
and to get a lift, they try and try again
they're so soaking wet, as the cold rain pours
but they won't give up, so they try some more

One man and his dog, standing in the sun
the rain has gone away, but they're not having, any fun
time is moving on, and the traffic keeps moving too
one man and his dog,don't know what to do

One man and his dog,standing in the dark
nightime has arrived, and the dog barks
they hear the haunting sound, of a night owl, hoot
one man and his dog, just don't feel so good

One man and his dog, standing through the night
the moon is slowing fading, they can see the morning light
but they are still there, on the same spot
the early traffic is moving, but they are not

One man and his dog, still trying to get a lift
now they're being passed, by workers, starting morning shifts
just when it seems, that they are totally out of luck
the one man and his dog, finally get picked up by a passing truck.

OPEN TOP JEEP

Cruising along, in my jeep, open topped
I want to keep going, do'nt want to stop
Chuck Berry, is on my radio
and I've got no particular place to go

The sun is beaming, from a deep blue sky
and the trees are flying by
a soft summer breeze, is blowing through my hair
I'm crusing along, without a care

I meet cars pulling caravans, or boats on trailers
and my radio plays Sun Is Shining, by Bob Marley and The Wailers
everybody seems to be heading for the coast
when the good weather is here, you got to make the most

But I'm not going to the beach today
in my jeep, I want to stay
I see men wearing sunglasses, and women with summer hats
cause summertime, is where it's at

People eating ice-cream, I pass
orthers are relaxing on the grass
there seems to be tents and kites everywhere
and a happy feeling, is in the air

As I drive through villages and towns
I see smiling faces, all around
there are festivals and some fairs
and street carnivals, here and there

Everyone loves the summertime
when the days are long, and the bright sun shines
I feel like driving, day and night, without any sleep
when I'm crusing along, in my open topped jeep.

PAINT ME A PICTURE

Painter,paint me a picture, of flowers so bright
some red, some yellow, purple and white
all growing in Spring, in a field of green
paint me the most colourful picture, ever seen

Painter, paint me a picture of little butterflies
flapping their wings, beneath a clear blue sky
paint me a picture, of long Summer days so hot
let it be,the most beautiful picture, you have got

Painter, paint me a picture, of golden brown leaves
slowly falling, down from the trees
rosey red apples, delicious and ripe
paint me a picture, of Autumn's delight

Painter, paint me a picture, of pure white snow
and a little Robin Redbreast, flying to and fro
paint me a picture, of a calm winters day
of snowballs and snowmen, and children at play

Painter, paint me a picture, of the world at peace
where people live in harmony, and all wars have ceased
make it a reality, not just a dream
painter, paint me the greatest picture that there has ever been.

PLENTY OF MORE FISH IN THE SEA

The lonely fish is so sad
he is as sad as he could be
because he has lost his love
but, there are plenty of more, fish in the sea

He recalls, the day they met
he was as happy as could be
but now, she has gone away
still, there are plenty of more fish in the sea

He met her one day in the shoal
the time was a quarter to three
they swam so loving, side by side
but there are plenty of more fish in the sea

They were so happy together
he felt, it was meant to be
but, she left him for another
still, there are plenty of more fish in the sea

She is really hooked on the orther, fish
and she clings, to him like bark to a tree
now the lonely fish is on his own
but, there are plenty of more fish in the sea

Perhaps, he will catch another, fish
and never set her free
he is really hopeful
cause there are plenty of more, fish in the sea.

PLAYING TO AN AUDIENCE OF ONE

He picks up his guitar in the usual way
stands on the stage, and prepares to play
takes out his plectrum, and begins to strum
but tonight, he is playing to an audience of one

He sings country with an American twang
and thinks of songs, over the years, he sang
there can't be, a country song he has'nt sung
but tonight, he is playing to an audience of one

He has sung Jim Reeves, Johnny Cash, the lot
he learned all the chords, himself, he never was caught
on his cowboy hat, the words, Son of a gun
but tonight, he is playing, to an audience of one

He has played all over the country, up and down
in every village and every town
his face is as familiar, as the setting sun
but tonight, he is playing, to an audience of one

He has sung in halls, clubs, and pubs as well
with so many memories, and stories to tell
he loves to play,and does it for fun
but tonight. he is playing, to an audience of one

He is a legend, in his own mind
he started singing back in, 1949
back then he was living with his dad and mum
but tonight, he is playing, to an audience of one

Now his old guitar is looking threadbare

it has seen better days, and been everywhere
just like it's owner,it's race has been run
and tonight, he is playing, to an audience of one

The one in question, is Willie Joe Mc Gee
and as usual, he's as drunk as he could be
the venue, The Hound And Gun
where tonight, the singer, is playing,to an audience of one

And now the night is old, the lights grow dim
the strings on his guitar are wearing thin
just like the singer,they are almost done
and tonight, he is playing, to an audience of one

The place is so quiet,empty and bare
everybody else, has gone else where
it is closing, time on the singer they have shuned
and tonight, he has played, to an audience of one.

P. T. O.

His name is, Paul Thomas Oxford
his initials are PTO
and he was called the turnover kid
everywhere he would go
he was told to turn over a new leaf
and turn over the page
all the slagging, he recieved
sometimes filled his heart with rage

He wished that he could change his name
but he did'nt know, what to
he was tired of being taunted
just like the boy named Sue
but unlike Sue in the song
Paul did'nt fight with his dad
he just got on with life
and accepted what he had

Paul was smart at school
and he was top of his class
each exam he did
he was sure to pass
when his school days were over
and to university he was sent
it was to Oxford University
that he naturlly went

But even as a student
the story was still the same
he was always being slagged
because of his name
orther students gave him apple turnovers to eat for lunch

but Paul resisted the temptation
to give them a punch

No matter what they'd say
however much, they teased
by saying things like,Turn over please
Paul would always be cool
he was the coolest person they ever saw
cause he knew how to behave himself
as he was studying law

And now he is a top judge
with a wig upon his head
yet he still remembers
what those orther boys said
when any of them appear before him
he soon lets them know
just how he feels at being taunted
about his initials PTO

So there's a lesson for everyone
be careful what you say
because those words that you use
might come back to haunt you some day
what lies in the future
no one really knows
but you just might meet somebody
whose initials, are PTO.

PUSHING UP DAISIES

I'm pushing up daisies
down here in the ground
it's nice and quiet
there is'nt a sound
I'm wearing my wooden overcoat
which is keeping me warm
at least down here
l won't come to any harm

l died one day
from a heart attack
the sun was shinning
but everything went black
l had a sweet in my mouth
and as l did suck it
l just keeled over
and kicked the bucket

They took me to the hospital
and put me in a morgue
they did a post mortem
to establish, why life, l did abort
they came to the conclusion
that in fact, l was dead
then my relatives arrived
and some prayers were said

l was put in a hearse
and driven slowly along
it was at this, point
l figured something was wrong
many came to my wake

well, at least one or two
l lay there so still
what else could l do?

Kind things were said, about me
l did'nt realise, that l was so good
l would have stayed on a bit longer
if only l could
but my old ticker went
and that was it
and so the dust
is what l bit

My funeral was big
or at least the church, was anyway
Father Mullin, did'nt have much to say
he got the mass over quickly
then out to my grave
and here in this hole in the ground
is where l was laid

l have nothing to do, here
but just lie about
some people would say
l never did anything else, no doubt
cause some reguarded me as been eternally lazy
but now l'm eternally
pushing up daises.

RAIN FALLING DOWNTOWN

It was the kind of day, where you would'nt chase your dog outside
never mind your cat
even ducks, were sheltering, it was as bad as that
there were floods on the roads, which resembled lakes
and the rain kept falling, it would'nt take a break

I looked out at the almost empty, streets in town
the wind, whisked plastic bags into the air, and tossed them around
black clouds, hung in the sky
it was such a miserable day, like a day to die

From my window in my high rise flat, l watched the scene below
what little traffic there was, moved so slow
l saw a woman standing in the doorway of a shop
trying to advoid the rain
and in the misty distance, l could see an almost empty train

The weather forecast, had got it wrong once more
it, said, there'd be sunny spells, but the rain continued to pour
l listened to my radio, all morning long
at least the DJs, played some happy songs

So stay indoors, was all l could do
and that, is what l did, the whole day through
then at night l closed my curtains, and went to bed
but still, l could see the rain falling, in my head.

REST IN PEACE

Rest in peace, take a seat
take the weight from off your feet
just relax, have a rest
that is what l suggest

Rest in peace, take a seat
close out the noise, that is on the street
because you want a little peace
when you rest, that's what you need

Do'nt answer the door, do,nt answer the phone
for all they know, you are not at home
pack up your cares, lock them away
they'll still be there, for another day

Kick out your worries, kick off your shoes
because that is, the thing to do
simply let the world drift by
just like a cloud, upon the sky

Put up your feet, pull down the blinds
and tonight, just ease your mind
think of nothing, but pretty things
like beautiful flowers, growing in spring

Bannish all problems, from your head
there will still, be problems, when you are dead
just let orthers take the heat
while you are still alive, simply rest, in peace

RIGHT THERE UNDER YOUR NOSE

Sometimes we're looking for an answer
an answer we can't find
and it really gets us down
simply blows your mind
but we keep on looking, searching high and low
when in fact the answer
is right there, under your nose

We are often too blind, to see the obvious
so we look all over the place
but all the time, the answer
is just in front of your face
still we can't seem to find,it
no matter where we go
but it's simply sitting
right, there under your nose

Far off fields look green
so we go, there and come back
still trying to find the needle
in that tall haystack
but the solution is much more simple
if we could only know
that the answer to the problem
is right, there under your nose

Sometimes we are going around in circles
getting nowhere, fast
trying to move forward
but living in the past
if we opened up our minds
we'd see the way to go

and we'd find the answer
right, there under your nose

Things seem so complicated
when in fact, they're not
in our search, we think we are getting colder
when, in fact we're hot
often that's how it is
that is how it goes
while the answer to the problem
is right, there under your nose.

SHOE SHINE MAN

Shoe shine man. shine my shoes
make them look, just brand new
they may be old, and down in the heels
but brighten them up, give them sex appeal

Shoe shine man, with your polish brush
I'm in no hurry, so you need'nt rush
I happened to walk this way, as I often do
but today I'll stop, for you to shine my shoes

Shoe shine man, I'm out of luck
I lost my job, driving a truck
my wife left me for another man
so brighten up my life, do the best, that you can

Shoe shine man, I hope you do'nt charge a lot
cause plenty of money, is something I have'nt got
but maybe I could pay, you by singing a song
I know a happy, little one, and it's not too long

Shoe shine man,I could play you a tune
I'm good on the tin whistle, and the spoons
you can have music while you work, you shine, I play
and perhaps more trade, will come your way

Shoe shine man, you are doing fine
polishing up, those shoes of mine
and I feel relaxed, sitting on this seat
the sun is shinning, as are the shoes on my feet.

SILENCE IS GOLDEN

If silence is golden, what colour is war
and does any one know, what we are fighting for?
all wars end the same way, in destruction, death and tears
it's been the same old story, down throughout the years

If silence is golden, what colour is peace
where people live in harmony, no fighting on the streets
and the sound of bombs and gunfire, don't fill the air
instead of people living in fear, for each orther, they do care

If silence is golden, what colour is hate?
to forgive, it is never too late
hate, is such a disaster
wounds, are created, too deep to be healed by plasters

If silence is golden, what colour is good?
where kindness, is spread just like it should
if this was a peaceful world, it would be great
instead of war and violence, death and hate

The answers to the questions, no one knows
but life can be as colourful, as a bright rainbow
still, people do their best, and their best is all, they can do
cause no, one wants to live their life, always being blue.

STAKE-OUT

In down town Drumstewart, on a sunny afternoon
there was a stake-out, in the Riverview salon
when Wild John Morris, and Mad Bill Mc Crea
held up the saloon staff, on a hot summers day

The cops quickly arrived, led by Sergeant Joe Brown
who ordered the gunmen, to put their weapons down
he told them, You've got five minutes to come out, or we are going in,
that is when the stake-out, really did begin

Morris and Mc Crea replied,There aint no way
we're not going out, we are in here to stay
you can say what you like, or do what you want
but force us out of here, is something you can't

The five minutes had come and gone, plus an hour or so
but still the gunmen, refused to go
Sergeant Brown was getting impatient, he did'nt know what to do
he had a problem, caused by the gunmen, numbered two

The saloon staff were worried, what was going to become of them
would they ever see, their loved ones again?
they pleaded with the gunmem, to spare them their lives
and let them go home, to their husbands and wives

The impasse went on, as did the time
and the sun had gone down, just after nine

darkness was falling,negoitations had failed
Morris and Mc Crea, were deterimed, not to go to jail

News quickly spread,and camera crews arrived
they wondered how many, of the saloon staff, were still alive
Sergeant Brown then got help,from the Chief of Police
who begged the gunmen, to have the workers released

The night had come and gone, and a new day dawned
but the stand-off, still went on
friends and relations of the staff, were concerned, the PM informed
then the army, was called upon

Tough soldiers, who had fought in the war
then surrounded, the Riverview bar
but still, Morris and Mc Crea, refused to give in
even though they knew, they just could'nt win

Minutes turned into hours, and hours into days
and in the saloon, the gunmen did stay
they were given one last chance, and then
if they still, did'nt come out,they'd never breathe again

Reporters from around the world, had descended on the town
to get the up-dates, and write them down
the story made the global front pages
on a situation, that went on for ages

Then at the eleventh hour, at eleven o clock at night

everybody, was filled with delight
cause the gunmen came out, reaching for the sky
they decided, it is better, to surrender than die

The saloon staff, were all alive and well
and what a story, they had to tell.

SUNNY SUMMERS SUNDAY

On a sunny summers Sunday
in the sunny summertime
we could go sailing on the sea
when the day is fine
you can bring your sunglasses
and I'll bring mine
some sunny summers Sunday
in the sunny summertime

Perhaps we could go fishing
in our Wellingtons and wets
we'll wade through the water
with our rods and fishing nets
we'd better bring bait
and some fishing line
on a sunny summers Sunday
in the sunny summertime

We could picnic in the park
and eat pickled eggs and plaice
we'd be properly positioned
so we'll have sunshine on our face
we won't overly induldge
under an oak tree or pine
on a sunny summers Sunday
in the sunny summertime

Maybe walking in the woods
would be a better, bet
we could pick delightful daises
or pretty violets
and if we don't get lost

we'll be home at nine
on a sunny summers Sunday
in the sunny summertime.

THAT MIDGE

I itched, l twitched,and l switched
from one, hand to another
l stratched, at the patch, and l hatched
a plan to catch, that midge, which was causing me bother
l swore, to the core, like never before
that l would get, it some way
but first, l cursed, cause the itch was getting worse
on that hot summers day

l sprayed, and l prayed, that the midge would go away
but it persisted
l thought, that l ought, to have caught, it
still, on staying, it insisted
l cried, and to catch it l tried, but it did hide
so deep in my hair
l moaned, and groaned, leave me alone
but the midge did'nt care

l sat, and spat, at the cat
in deep frustration
l shook, and looked, up a book
on how to end, my situation
the book was brown, and l frowned, as l looked around
for some solution
but l was enraged, as each stage, of each page
caused me more confusion

l was going insane, but thought again, then walked in the rain
and the midge was gone

l felt great relief, indeed, but l do believe
l should have thought,of that, all along
but as they say, anyway, every day
all's well that ends well.

THE APPLE TREE

I was sitting under an apple tree
one evening in September
the autumn sun was shinning,
on a day l always will remember
an apple hit me on the head
which made my head feel sore
and when l started eating the apple
it was rotten to the core

So l climbed, the apple tree
with it's apples red
to get a better, one
than that, which hit me on the head
l went from branch to branch
to get the apple l desired
it was when l got to the top
that l felt, so very tired

Then l grew drowsy
and lay down on a branch, which was thick
and so l fell asleep
it happened very quick
l dreamt, l was in the garden of eden
along with Adam and Eve
and they warned me not to pick an apple
from a certain tree

The garden of eden was beautiful
life, there was sweet
there were angels above, me
and lovely flowers at my feet
it was simply paradise, and there were many apple trees

l was feeling hungry
so l thought l'd try one, and see

But l picked from the wrong, tree
and just as before
the apple that l picked
was rotten to the core
then God, spoke to me
his voice, was loud and clear
he said, You have done wrong
so you must leave here,

When l woke from my dream
the moon was shinning bright
the sky had darkened
cause day, had turned into night
and as l climbed down, from the tree
to go back home
l still wanted, an apple
but every single one, was gone.

THE BIRD FLEW BLUES

I had the flu, what could I do
whenever my bird flew?
she went away, one cold spring day
and now I have the bird flew blues

She said I was bringing her down
so she left town
she left me nothing, but the flu
and now she's gone, I'm all alone
with these bird flew blues

I had the sniffs and sneezes
coughs and wheezes
I felt so miserable, through and through
it was as if I was cursed, but now I feel even worse
with these bird flew blues

She was my only one, my ray of sun
now all I have, is rain, the whole day through
as the rain continues to pour
every day, I get more
of these bird flew blues

I begged her please, got down on my knees
please, do'nt say we are through
but she took off like a plane
in the pouring rain
and left, me these bird flew blues

She said, she had to get out
because if, she stayed about
I might give her the flu

but now I'm feeling stronger
I have the flu no longer
instead, I've got the bird flew blues.

CAR BOOT SALE

I went to a car boot sale, the orther week
cause a boot for my car, is what l did seek
when l arrived, what a surprise
there were boots of every colour and size

Black boots, white boots, red and green
every shade, there's ever been
yellow boots, purple pink and blue
so very many, were in view

Round boots, oblong boots and some square
every kind was gathered there
there really was, such a choice
boots for cars driven by girls, and by boys

There were all ages of people, young and old
though the sun did'nt shine, and the day was cold
but at least the weather did stay dry
as customers arrived, some boots to buy

There was'nt anybody, whom l did know
with the exception, of Mickey Joe
Mickey is a friend of mine
he goes to car boot sales all the time

He had boots to buy, and boots to sell
at the car boot, business he is doing well
he always makes a pound or two
and that is what he likes to do

When l saw Mickey, we stopped for a chat
and at the end of the day that was that

by the time we had finished talking, the boots were all gone
there was nothing to do, but just go home

The next time, to a car boot sale l do go
l hope l won't meet Mickey Joe
cause l did'nt achieve,what l set out to do
and that was to buy a car boot or two

Now all of the papers, l do scan
looking for car boot sales all over the land
I'd go any where, near or far
in order to buy a boot for my car

So if you see me comming, don't stand in my way
because this, time l don't want any delays
a boot for my car, is what l must find
of any colour and any kind.

THE CAR IN FRONT IS A TOWING

The car in front is a towing
it's towing the one at the back
and in between, there's a rope which used to be green
but now it has faded to black

The car at the back has broken down
that's why it is on tow
it gave up along the way, and it seemed to say
I just don't want to go

It was built a long time ago
back in nineteen thirdy two
it was a lovely car, back before the war
when it was shiny and new

With it's chrome bumpers
it was built to last
but I do fear, it's best years
are all in the past

And now, it has grown tired and weary
it is showing it's age, and some rust
the tyres have worn thin, the boot is letting in
and the seats are covered in dust

It has gone long, past it's sell-by date
though it has had many glorious years
it was one of the very best
but now, the time has come for it to be laid to rest
still, only the rain, will shed any tears

So the car in front is a towing it

to it's final resting place
nothing lasts for ever, everything must die
parting is such sweet sorrow
time to say, goodbye.

THE CROOKED BRIDGE

By the crooked bridge, over the crooked stream
there lives a crooked man in a house of green
at the end of a crooked lane, which has a crooked ditch
stands the crooked house, by the crooked bridge

The crooked little man, sits by the fire
and up the crooked chimney, the smoke rises higher
he has a funny little dog, which he calls Midge
and they both live, by the crooked bridge

He smokes his crooked pipe,while sitting on his crooked chair
at the clock on the mantlepiece, he sits and stares
when the clock strikes one, his right, eye does twitch
that crooked little man, by the crooked bridge

When the night arrives, he lays down on his crooked bed
and upon a crooked pillow, he rests his tired old head
he turns out the crooked light, with a crooked switch
in his crooked house, by the crooked bridge

Early in the morning, he hears a rooster crow
then he opens up the crooked curtains, on his crooked window
he gets into his worn clothes, which could do with a stitch
that crooked little man, by the crooked bridge

He takes funny little dog, out for a walk each day
and in the shade of a crooked tree, has a rest along the way

he stratches his balding head, because he has an itch then he pauses, gazing into the water, at the crooked bridge.

THE FLEA PIT

Welcome to the flea pit, sit back and enjoy the show
but when you are leaving, be careful how you go
cause there are broken floorboards, which are hard to see
as the lights are not working, so careful, you'd better be

Some of the seats are'nt so comfortable, that, I must admit
there are dodgy, ones, so be careful where you sit
a few of the backs may be broken, and cover torn
because the seats are getting old, and well worn

We don't want any disasters, apart from those on the screen
tonights film is The Towering Inferno, at least it was to have been
but last night, the film got entangled, when our projector broke down
we did'nt have an engineer, so we had to phone around

When at last, we got one, he said the film was beyond repair
so we had to have a change of programe, I hope you are aware
instead, we've got Tom and Jerry, it is a cartoon
we hope to have another Towering Inferno, film, pretty soon

Hopefully, this won't spoil your enjoyment, and I apologize

it's not what you came to see,l realise
but for now, it's the best we can do
and once again, l apologize to you

l'm sorry to tell, you, that you can't have any refunds
still, Tom and Jerry are such good fun
and as l said at the start, enjoy the show
don't forget, on your way out, be careful how you go.

THE HALFWAY HOUSE

The Halfway House, is between here and there
you are sure to see, it if you are going any where
they'll sell you whiskey, and some beer
in that house, halfway, between there and here

They would brighten up your life if you are feeling dull
your glass won't be half empty, but half full
and you will leave, filled with cheer
in the house halfway, between there and here

The barman, is so jolly, he'll tell you a joke
and he really is, such a friendly bloke
but his jokes are'nt dirty, let me make that clear
in the the house halfway, between there and here

The barmaid who helps him, is a lovely blonde
she is good at her job, though she has'nt been there long
cause she's only been working, half a year
in the house halfway, between there and here

Each Friday night, they have a sing-song
and if you like, you can sing along
even then, the drinks are'nt dear
in the house halfway, between there and here

There's guitar Willie, he'll give you a tune
and if requested, he would play the spoons
but when he does, people hold their ears
in the house halfway, between there and here

At happy hour, the drinks are half price
and the food they serve, is really nice
but if you are half cut, you'll be shown the door, l fear
in the house halfway, between there and here.

THE RETURN OF A LOCAL HERO

He returns today, in shinning glory
everybody is there, wanting to hear his story
about how he got to the top, and found fame
yet when he left, few knew his name

It is a case of, local boy comes good
though very few, thought he ever would
some even say, in bygone days he was bad
but now he's the biggest hero, they ever had

When he left town, not so long ago
nobody bothered to watch him go
still, now hundreds of people, have lined the streets
they have come to see him, he's the one they want to meet

There's a brass band waiting to welcome him home
and his father, is even playing trombone
a banner has been erected, tied to lamposts
and tonight, to him, they will raise a toast

He never thought it would be this way
cause he was poor, in his younger days
running around with his clothes in stitches
he really has gone, from rags to riches

He has simply become, an overnight sensation
cause now he's known, all over the nation
but it's not easy, staying at the top
though he hopes his popularity, will never drop

He's been on tv, and radio

now people recongnize him,where ever he goes
newspapers have printed his photograph
and girls, flock around him for his autograph

Today he'll be comming home on the evening train
he is looking forward, to seeing his parents again
his brother Jim, will be there too
as will his sister, Peggie Sue

Even a few of his old pals, are waiting to see him today
cause they have missed him, since he went away
and lots of people, he has never even known
are waiting to greet him, like he was one of their own

Nothing ever happens, in this sleepy little town
that is why there are so many people now standing around
because they never had a local hero before
his parents have been inundated, with callers at their door

His uncle John, has even flown over from the USA
just to welcome him home today
and his long lost cousins, are there too
some of them, he never even knew

He'll be met at the station, by his brother Jim
who will take him home, then the fun will begin
he can't drive himself, so he has'nt got a car
but he has got talent, and now he's a star

Drinks will flow, and, Well Done, will too
there'll be partying, the whole night through

photos will be taken, many cameras will flash
for the local hero, with plenty of cash.

THE NAKED CHEF

The naked chef, wore no clothes
everything, was exposed
he walked around, in the nude
every time, that he cooked food

Because his kitchen was so hot
he took off his clothes, he shed the lot
from his hat, down to his shoes
that is what he used to do

The bacon he cooked, was always streaked
if some one complained, he'd turn the orther cheek
he used to think clothes got in the way
so he cooked in the nude, every day

His resturant was in the back streets of Rome
and he always cooked alone
people from all over Italy, from Milan to Naples
would dine in his resturant, when they were able

Even people from France
used to taste his meals, when they got the chance
his pizzas were the best, they used to say
that is why so many custommers, went his way

But there were those who questioned, if he really should
be allowed to cook, in just his birthday suit
and then the authorities, forced him to close
simply because, he would'nt wear any clothes

So he moved on, and set up, somewhere else

and he continues to cook, all by himself
when he is cooking, he still, wears no clothes, right or left
so he is still known, as the naked chef.

THE RAIN HOUSE

All the games, we would play, in the rain, house
on a wet and windy day, in the rain, house
out in the country, far from town
when the rain, came pouring down
the only shelter for miles around
was the rain, house

An old thatched cottage,made of stone, was the rain, house
standing there on it's own, the rain, house
you were my princess, l was your king
l did'nt have a crown, you did'nt have a ring
still and all, we had everything
in the rain, house

We'd hear the rain crash, against the windows glass, in the rain, house
many happy hours we would pass, in the rain house
down the chimney, the wind would blow
how the old doors rattled so
but still, we did'nt want to go
from the rain, house

Many's a wet day we did meet, in the rain, house
when from the rain, shelter we would seek, in the rain,house
and it really kept us dry
when those black clouds covered the sky
and time, just seemed to fly
in the rain, house

You were six and I was seven, in the rain, house
but we had a little bit of heaven, in the rain, house
now that seems so long ago
the rain still falls, and the wind still blows
perhaps some, day, we'll both go
back to the rain, house

Maybe once again, we'll have fun, in the rain, house
when, in the rain, we will run, to the rain, house
and we could relive old happy times
when I was yours and you were mine
perhaps then, the sun will shine
in the rain, house.

THE RIVER

The river flows gently by, it's waters rippling in the wind
l wonder where it ends, l wonder where it begins
lt weaves it's way through town and country
like a snake in the grass
sometimes flowing slowly, sometimes flowing fast

Cattle graze happily on it's banks, but it does'nt care
it just keep on flowing, it's secrets, it won't share
fishermen prod it's bed, hoping for a bite
children throw stones into it, laughing with delight

The river meanders on and on,
morning noon and night
it's waters are ilumated by the sun in daytime
and in the dark, by the bright moonlight

ln the summertime, when the weather is dry
the river can just be a trickle, like a tear from a giants eye
when there is rainy weather, it sometimes overflows
but come the winter time, its chilly waters have often froze

Still, it keeps on flowing, year in, year out
and it will still be going, when we're not about.

THE SCARECROW

Sticks and stones won't break my bones
cause I'm made of straw and wood
I'm standing lonely, in this field
and I'd leave, it if I could

There is a hat upon my head, that the farmer used to wear
now it's only second hand, and I don't think, that's fair
the only orther, thing I'm wearing, is a shabby old coat
and the chances of it keeping me warm
are, to say the least, remote

I'm anchored on a pole, which is stuck in the ground
maybe I'd scare the birds away, if I could move my arms around
but unfortunatly, I can't, which does'nt make any sense at all
sometimes, the birds scare me, when I listen to them call

One day a bird landed on my head, and my straw, it did peck
I could'nt shake, my head to chase, it
cause I can't move, my neck
all I could do, was stand there, though it hurt me so
that bird must have thought, what a silly scare crow

Those birds keep on comming, they never seem to stop
I'll be glad to get out of here, when the farmer lifts the crops

this is such a thankless, job, l don't be paid a penny
and as for a reward, l never do get any.

THE TRAVELLER

I'm a traveller on the road, living on beans
following the sun, and chasing my dreams
l am always on the go, moving from town to town
aint nobody, going to slow me down

Do'nt pay rates, do'nt pay any rent
do'nt know, where l'm going, could'nt tell, you where l went
l'm as free as a bird, like an animal untamed
l just keep moving on, and no, one knows my name

Aint got any worries, and don't have any plans
all l have is a tent, and l pitch it where l can
in a quiet feild, somewhere, when the stars are shinning bright
l lay down my head, and rest for the night

Then early next day, l'm on the road again
always travelling on, in the sun and rain
l have passed through many towns, been to many places
seen so many people, but can't remember faces

Some say l am foolish, to live my life this way
but on the open road, is where l want to stay
l do'nt really care, about what orthers do
life is short, and we are all, just travelling through

So l've got to keep moving, like a flowing stream
following the sun, and chasing my dreams
l'm not going to stop, till my time has come to go
cause life on the road, is the only life l know.

THE UMBRELLA MAN

There's an umbrella man, on down the street
he sells every kind, of umbrella, that you could need
all shapes and sizes, he sells them all
and you can buy them there, at his umbrella stall

He has umbrellas which are black, and some green
and every colour of the rainbow, in between
even multi-coloured, umbrellas and polka dots
and when it rains, they'll catch every drop

There are umbrellas for each and every occasion
any event, or situation
umbrellas to protect you from the rain
and orthers give protection from the sun
the umbrella man, sells every one

He sells golf, umbrellas, which are big and strong
beach, umbrellas, you can sit under all day long
fashion, umbrellas, for the ladies just for show
umbrellas which go high, orthers stay low

Some football, umbrellas, to take to the match
they will give you full protection, while you watch
folding, umbrellas, which fit into your pocket
and pointed, umbrellas, that look like mini rockets

Umbrellas to take to the river, when you go to fish
every kind of umbrella, that you could wish
umbrellas for every woman, and every man
they are all there, at the umbrella stand

There are umbrellas for children, which have pictures of frogs
he even sells unbrellas, especially for dogs
as far as umbrellas go, he just can't be beat
that umbrella man, on down the street.

THE UPSIDE DOWN WATCH

The upside down watch, was really upside down
it's numbers did'nt add up
cause they were the wrong way around
the back was at the front and the front was at the back
the hands were the colours of the rainbow
instead of being black

The watch did'nt tick
it just went tock
and no matter which way you looked at it
it looked more like a clock
it was'nt made in Switzerland
as it was made in Hong Kong
and on the day it was assembled
everything just went wrong

The factory was in darkness, because of a power cut
workers could'nt get parts for the watch
as the suppliers were all shut
due to the lack of light
the workers had to use a match
those were the conditions
when they made, the upside down watch

The power cut was caused, by an electricity strike
electricity workers wanted a watch on retirement
but they were being offered a bike
by the time retirement age would come around
a bike would'nt be of any use
the management offered a compromise
which the workers refused

Back at the watch, factory
where the watches were made
workers were being paid off
even though, they were'nt being paid
there was'nt any money to pay them with
as they were'nt making any watches
many months had passed,
since the last dispatches

Times were tough, at the watch factory it's true
in old Hong Kong,back in nineteen thirdy two
unlike the upside down watch, the factory went
sold to a company which makes boots
but as the saying goes
it's an ill wind, which blows no good

The watch became a collectors item
very much in demand
because of it's upside face
and multicoloured hands
it is now worth a fortune
bought by a millionair called Joe
he wears it every where
even though it still does'nt go.

THERE IS SNOW

There is snow on the mountains
and down by the glen
some more in the valleys
and up around the bend
there is snow in feilds
where cows usually go
and everywhere you look, there is snow

There is snow on rooftops
and on many window sills
folk sit round a fire
out of the cold winter chill
inside, it is warm, outside, it is five below
and everywhere you look, there is snow

There is snow in the park
where children do play
they're throwing snowballs
and pulling home made sleighs
they are well wrapped up
as the cold wind blows
and everywhere you look, there is snow

There is snow in the forest
where trees, grow so tall
and down their branches
the snow softly falls
reindeers footprints, show where they go
and everywhere you look, there is snow

There is snow in cities and in towns
where people wearing, hats, coats and gloves

are walking around
there's a disruption to traffic, it has to go slow
and everywhere you look. there is snow

There is snow in the meadows
and down by the lake
where summer people go
when taking a break
there is snow in the garden
where flowers usually grow
and everywhere you look, there is snow

There is snow on the farm
up lanes and up hills
but the farmer has to keep going
to pay his winter bills
it is that time of year, as we all know
when everywhere you look, there is snow

As we patiently wait, for spring to arrive
through the long winter months
somehow we got to survive
survive frozen fingers, and frozen toes
as everywhere you look, there is snow

The snow covers all of the land
like a gaint white blanket
Gods winter gift to man
and like it or not, we are stuck with it so
cause everywhere you look, there is snow.

THREADMILL STREET

Everything happens on Threadmill Street
all kinds of people, there you'll meet
every sort of colour, class and creed
all live together on Threadmill Street

You can sing in a choir, or play in a band
be a funny clown, or even Superman
dance to a fiddle if you are light on your feet
you can do it all on Threadmill Street

You can shop till you drop in the local store
they have everything you want, and even more
and for the children, there are lots of sweets
nobody goes hungry, on Threadmill Street

Every summertime they hold a carnival
at one end of the street, upon the hill
and the carousel, sure is a treat
you'll have lots of fun, on Threadmill Street

Then in the winter, when the snow does fall
you can ski down the hill , or throw snowballs
while the old folk by the fireside,enjoy the heat
everyone is catered for, on Threadmill Street

But if ever you are there in the spring
when flowers bloom and robins sing
it's a wonderful place to be indeed
life is a breeze, on Threadmill Street

There is a cinema on the street, open 24 hours
you can go right in out of the showers

they show a film for free, once a week
entertainment is fine on Threadmill Street

If things are'nt going right,and you are feeling down
you could do much worse, than come to town
just pass the boats,of which you'll see a fleet
then turn to the right, onto Threadmill Street

You can stay,for as long as you care
friendly people you'll meet there
you'll soon get into the groove, into the beat
cause you can't go wrong on Threadmill Street

The street is long,straight and wide
with brightly coloured buildings on either side
of course it is always clean and neat
it's a wonderful life on Threadmill Street

You can have a drink in the Harbour Bar
that is where you will get, whiskey in the jar
then a little nightcap, makes the day complete
just sheer perfection, is Threadmill Street.

TIDE ME OVER

Tide me over, when I'm all at sea
when I am drowning, come and rescue me
in stormy waters, keep me afloat
you can be saviour, my lifeboat

Tide me over, when the cold wind roars
and the hungry wolves, are howling at my door
be my companion, in my hour in need
I'll be contented, if you are there with me

Tide me over,when I'm in dispair
when I'm reaching out, but no, one is there
and I'm down on my luck, and down on my knees
when I feel uncomfortable, come and comfort me

Tide me over,when the rain pours down
and the sky is grey, there's darkness all around
when I need some shelter, you can shelter me
you can be my umbrella, my protective tree

Tide me over,in the blackest night
when at the end of the tunnel, there is no light
and the big old moon has lost it's shine
you can be a torch, to this heart of mine

Tide me over, when I've lost my way
cause I'll need some guidance, come that day
and beneath my feet there is stoney ground
when I'm feeling desperate, wanting to be found

Tide me over,when I do'nt belong
when nothing is right, and everything is wrong

and a fish out of water, is what I am
when I need some help, from a helping hand

Tide me over, when I'm all alone
when I've got no friends, all my friends are gone
and a lonesome star, on me does shine
tide me over, be a friend of mine.

TOM DICK AND HARRY

Tom Dick and Harry, are the top comedy team
in halls, clubs and theatres,they can be seen
they have audiences rolling in the aisles, and venues packed
everybody laughs at their jokes
even the old lady at the back

Tom is the eldest of the two
Harry, his younger brother
in the first half of the show,
Tom tells the jokes, then Harry does the orther
they do a double act, for the grand finale
and their jokes, they write themselves
with a little help from sister Sally

It truly is a family show,their jokes suit everyone
from the very oldest, to the very young
there's nothing rude or offensive
in the jokes they tell
that's why they can go to any venue
they do private, functions as well

They do births and marriages
christenings, and confirmations
and they are always in demand
all across the nation
they do birthday and farewell parties
and even for divorces, they get requests
cause when it comes to cheering people up
they are the very best

Their father, Mick Dick, was a comedian many years ago
lots of people went to see his one man show
and his shows were well enjoyed, by each and every one
then when he retired, the act was taken over by his sons

From the very moment, they go on stage
you can hear the laughing start
all kinds of people go to see them
even those with a broken heart
doctors, lawyers, rich and poor
all guaranted to have a laugh,
that much is for sure

If you are feeling down in the dumps
or broken hearted
if from your lover, you have just parted
even if nothing is going right and everything is wrong
then to their show, you should go along
cause they'll certainly cheer you up, no end
you won't have a frown on your face, ever again
you'll be bursting your sides, as happy as Larry
whenever you go to see, Tom Dick and Harry.

U. B. DUNNE

Here lies the body of U. B. Dunne
his days are numbered, his race has been run
he died one day at a quarter to three
and that was the end, of old U.B.

He out-stayed his welcome, he was one hundred and four
when he went knocking on heavens door
but he was well liked, by those he knew
he did have friends, at least one or two

He worked on the railway, laying down tracks
and there was a hump, upon his back
because every day, his back was bent
all those years, on the railway he spent

His wrinked skin, was as tough as leather
being out, in all kinds of weather
rain, hail, snow and sun
a dedicated worker, was U. B. Dunne

He worked so hard, all his life
that he never found time, to find a wife
he just lived for his job, and a pint of beer
that's how it was, till his final years

Then he took a fever,which was so strong
after that, he did'nt last, very long
no matter what medicine, his doctor gave him
nothing at all, could really save him

So here he is, old U. B.
his days are numbered, as you can see
he died away back, in nineteen sixty one
and that was the end, of U. B. Dunne.

UNCLE TOM

He married his niece, on an island in Greece
one morning, in the month of June
it was a sunny day, when they went away
to New York, on their honeymoon

He was sixty four, or even more
she, was only twenty nine
but she did'nt care, that he had greying hair
or, that he was always drinking wine

Her mother did'nt approve, she said her daughter would lose
and told, her she should find another
she warned it was'nt right, and though she tried with all her might
she could'nt stop her daugher, marrying her brother

They lived in a cottage by the coast
and for breakfast they had beans on toast
together, with a cup of tea
when it came to dinner time
he would down a bottle of wine
and eat fish, which he caught in the sea

Years came and went, and he grew old and bent
all he could do, was watch the shadows on the wall
he could'nt fish anymore, so he'd sit by the cottage door
and listen, to the seagulls call
When he became ninety seven,
the Lord, called him up to heaven
and he was laid to rest in peace

all his friends were sad, and everything that he had went to his widow, who was also his niece.

UP TO THE EYES

Up to the eyes, up to the ears
up to the neck, deep in fear
head full of problems, heart full of sorrow
thinking about, what will happen tomorrow

Worries afoot, trouble at hand
looking ahead, though nothing is planned
down on your luck, down on your knees
down in the mouth, and begging please

Heart full of joy, eyes full of glee
face full of smiles, for the whole world to see
head full of happiness, mindfull of all that is good
everything's fine, things are as they should

A song in the heart, a spring in the step
good times to remember, and not forget
a handful of hope, for many happy times
clear are the thoughts, clear is the mind

Such are the emotions, people go through
sometimes happy, orther times blue
never knowing, what will happen next
living a life, of emotions mixed.

WAIT TILL I TELL YOU

Wait till l tell, you, do'nt walk away
stay here a while on this fine spring day
the birds are singing high in the trees
wait till l tell, you, spend a little time with me

Flowers are in bloom up on Daffodil Hill
wheels are turning, down at the old mill
in feilds of green, lambs of white are at play
the sun is shinning, on this fine spring day

My story is true, and my story is sweet
it's been a long time, since last we did meet
but l hope, that you're back to stay
l have so much to tell you on this fine spring day

Things are so different now, from before
they just are'nt the same anymore
some of our old friends died, orthers went away
but worry you not, on this fine spring day

Down on the farm, they are sowing the seeds
to grow some crops, the cattle to feed
the tractor and plough, have turned over the clay
things are moving, on this fine spring day

Gardeners are busy, growing food for human kind
while that sun in the sky, continues to shine
it is cheaper to grow your own,than in a shop , have to pay
and now is the time, on this fine spring day

But wait till l tell, you, and l fool you not

I've so much to talk about, in fact quite a lot
I hope you can listen to what I have to say
so lend me your ears, on this fine spring day

My mind sometimes wanders, and I do forget
just what I was talking about, and it happens yet
to tell you the truth, I've forgotten what I was going to say
still, nice to meet again, on this fine spring day

I've enjoyed your company, and hope you stay around
do'nt be in a hurry to get out of town
call again, next time you are passing this way
and we'll have another little chat, on a fine spring day.

WALKING CAN BE DANGEROUS

Walking can be dangerous, on a windy day
whenever there's a storm, trees begin to sway
slates on rooftops move,and then they blow away
walking can be dangerous, on a windy day

Strange sounds are heard, which normally we don't hear
noises, when out walking, that can cause fear
like the haunting howling sound, of the wind in your ears
walking can be dangerous,even when the day is clear

Lamposts shake, and telephone poles do too
as the wind increases, whereas gently, it once blew
storm clouds gather in the sky, and not just a few
walking can be dangerous,it really is true

Items go flying through the air, all kinds of things
not just planes and birds and kites with strings
flying objects are hazardous, many problems they bring
walking can be dangerous,in winterime or spring

When the wind is blowing strong, it can lift you off your feet
along a country road, or on a city street
if it knocks you down, your misery is complete
walking can be dangerous, it truly can indeed

So on a windy day, it is better to stay indoors
whenever you hear, the strong winds roar
and warning signs,you'd better not ignore
walking can be dangerous,that much is for sure.

WHERE THE WILD ROSES GROW

Wild roses, take me back to a time
when l was young, and life was fine
living in the country, where the wild roses grow
it does'nt seem, so long ago

Walking over fields of freedom
on a carpet of buttercups and dasies
lying by a sleepy stream
when l was feeling lazy
playing hide and seek in the meadow
where the grass grew tall
happy times, that l recall

Fetching water, from a well
lots of stories, l could tell
footing turf, in sunny weather
then playing games, among the heather

Riding on pigs backs, and holding on to their ears
speeding down a hill, on a home made cart
using my feet, to steer
being scared, by the call of the corncrake, in the night
playing football, by the bright moonlight

Hearing crickets, in a chimney breast
those were the days, they were the best
walking to school in the frost and snow
being rapped by the teacher, for being slow

Jumping over bales of hay, when the hay was being baled
how it made me laugh, it never failled

milking cows in an old barn
listening to old, folks telling yarns

Going out,for a country ramble
being pricked, by those thorny brambles
gathering blackberries, stealing from apple trees
climbing stone walls, getting cut knees

Still it does'nt seem so long ago
since I was living in the country
where the wild roses grow.

YELLOW DREAMS

There's a yellow moon shinning tonight
and it gives off a yellow light
it shines on yellow rivers and yellow streams
l can see it all in my yellow dreams

There's a yellow bird , flying overhead
while a yellow man sleeps in his bed
in his yellow house at the top of the hill
and in his garden, grow some daffodils

l'm standing on a yellow bridge
watching the river flowing fast
while on the road a yellow jeep drives past
l look around wearing my yellow coat
and on the lake' see a yellow boat

Moving on, l pass a yellow bush
taking my time, being in no rush
there's a yellow balloon, floating on the nightime breeze
high above, the yellow trees

l walk on some more, with yellow shoes on my feet
then gradually enter, Yellow Street
and see yellow windows and yellow doors
all with numbers starting with four

Finally l arrive home and sit on my yellow seat
then take my yellow shoes from off my feet
on a yellow cabinet, sits my tv
out of my yellow cup, l drink some tea

I read the papers I've just read
before trudging off to bed
on my yellow pillow, I lay down my head for the night
after turning off, my yellow light

That is when, I have my yellow dreams
of yellow rivers and yellow streams
and so, I dream the night away
at the end, of another yellow day

When I awaken, in the morn
all my yellow dreams are gone
then I see everything in black and white
until I go to bed again, at night

Then I have my yellow dreams once more
just like I had the night before
yellow visions in my head
as I lie sleeping, in my yellow bed

SEE YOU LATER

I'Il see you later
hopefully, sometime soon
in the not too distant future
beneath the shinning moon
down a quiet country lane
under an old oak tree
I will be waiting there for you
if you'll be there for me

In the stillness of the night
we could have a rendezvous
when the world has gone to bed
and there is only, me and you
we'll be serenaded by the sound
of a Nightingale in a tree
singing it's sweet song of love
for only you and me

And we can take our time
because time will be our own
doing what we like
when we're together, all alone
and we'll feel the gentle touch
of the nightime breeze
blowing softly our way
just, for you and me

Then we will sit down together
on a spot, both soft and dry
while that big old silver moon
smiles on us, from in the sky
and what happens after that

no prying, eyes will see
it'll be our secret in the night
to be shared by only, you and me.

ISBN 142510478-9

9 781425 104788